Voyages of the Heart

John Caldwell

Poetry Series
by John Caldwell

A SYNTHESIS FROM DOGWOOD RIDGE
RUSTLINGS ABOVE SAURURUS HOLLOW
VOYAGES OF THE HEART
BEFORE THE GARDEN GROWS WILD

Voyages of the Heart

Appalachia and Beyond

John Caldwell

Caldwell Publications † Dogwood Ridge

VOYAGES OF THE HEART
by John Caldwell

Copyright © 1985 by
Caldwell Publications † Dogwood Ridge
P. O. Box 5332, Arlington, VA 22205

Library of Congress Catalog Card Number: 85-73047
ISBN Hardbound: 0-932777-01-5

Editor: Genevieve A. Brune

Printed in the United States of America
First Printing: September 1985

DONALD WERNSING BRUNE

A TRUE FRIEND
WHOSE EARLY DEATH BRINGS
A TERRIBLE SENSE OF URGENCY
TO MY LIFE AND MY LOVE OF LIFE

VOYAGES OF THE HEART

The places that we go and the experiences they bring are all seen first and last through the heart. The heart, or the soul as you will, seems to be in control of what images become to us beyond our waking, dreaming, dying.

Voyages of the heart are the imprints life leaves on us and what we reflect onto others and into time. Most outstanding in my life travels are those few true friendships which I treasure more and more above any other measure. For with each dawning day I sense them, one by one, slipping away.

Here, my song is sung to the best pal anyone could ever wish for, to our searoads together and life points apart. Though grief follows me in seeing him to his destiny, my love for him and the values that we share remain untarnished.

John Caldwell
Dogwood Ridge, Virginia

♥ ♡ ♥ ♡ ♥ ♡ ♥ ♡ ♥ ♡ ♥ ♡ ♥ ♡ ♥

♠ ♤ ♠ ♤ ♠ ♤ ♠ ♤ ♠ ♤ ♠ ♤ ♠ ♤ ♠

RELEARNING KNOTS   69

♥ ♡ ♥ ♡ ♥ ♡ ♥ ♡ ♥ ♡ ♥ ♡ ♥ ♡ ♥

♠ ♤ ♠ ♤ ♠ ♤ ♠ ♤ ♠ ♤ ♠ ♤ ♠ ♤ ♠

Heart Strings

"To the trembling girls who fed lusty young appetites
strong, feisty drinks under palms swaying gently..."

O' LET ME PLAY MY VIOLIN

O' let me play my violin
O' let me time it to the flutters of my heart
O' let me play the songbird in your throat
O' let me draw the bow quiveringly
And paint the tremble on your lips
O' let me! Let me! Let me!

O' let me play my violin
"O' fairer than the fairest," I will sing to you
"More beautiful than the most beautiful."
O' let me die inside your tender grasp
Nursed close upon your milk white breast
To sing and play for you, my soul
This will be heaven enough!

AN EASTER THOUGHT

To see the world through only
    a third of an eye
Intentionally covered by
    an old straw hat
    an easter bonnet
    a helmet
    blades of grass
    bleeding arm
    sweaty palm
Drowning in my lover's breast
Is to be found!
Knowing I am safe from all harm
Not being afraid anymore
Bubbling over with joy
Throwing my half-empty basket
    in the face of the world
Saying I don't care for
    anything or more
That I am loved alone for myself
And that's all that matters
In these later days.

SAY

Say you were loved by someone
Say you were loved by me
    If you needed one to
    Name who once loved you
Say that someone.....was me.

THIS ILLICIT ECSTASY

A dusty darkened road,
A softened summer sky,
A hard red highland path,
And this illicit ecstasy.

The blue above the trees,
The rise of laughter, cries of joy
Looking straight up, pillows soft
From this illicit ecstasy—
Riding this spinning world
And glad I didn't refuse it!

Her emerald eyes said, "*Yes!*"
Her rose hands caressed and held
Her full ruby lips kissed life
Into illicit ecstasy!

Illicit but strong as
The strengths of two sealed in
One embrace forever
Bolting doors against a
World of haste, learning this
Illicit ecstasy was Life.

O' give me your emerald eyes,
O' give me your rosy pink hands,
O' give me your full ruby lips,
To repaint the sounds of ecstasy!

BECAUSE TOMORROW

Because tomorrow she may change
Or I shall change and the way we view
Each other may never be the same again,
I thought that I must tell her in some way
What was on my mind today,
How I had known her and admired her
Held her high above all others, and
I asked myself just why and knew instantly
It was because she had never changed,
She could be depended on
Like the tides on shore
Or a glimmering star laughing along,
Just a little girl being herself
Wanting to live so much and
Some would discourage her, I knew
And I realized that this was a life story
Never truly told, revealing
God's best work
His greatest art and gift to man
Like so many gleamings
Of the summer sun off the mountaintop
Much more valued than heaven's wedding bed.
I had nothing to offer as a complement
To such beautiful magnificence
Not even words, soft enough, true enough.
My soul is cheap for the beauty it could preserve
And my need to protect her right to be
Goes hurting.

THINGS TO DO TODAY

Tonight is like all nights
For that's when I'm alone
With your photograph
Your eyes stare silently
I try to talk to them
But then I realize
It's just a photograph
That I am talking to
Still it's comforting
Just to have your eyes
Looking down on me

They never say a thing
I try to explain
What it was that I
Wanted to tell you
In that old churchyard
Where now I never go
To say what was not said
That which I never had
The chance to say before
Fate never made a way
For me to say it right

When on this night
I count all the
"Things To Do Today"
Tomorrow, I am at a
Loss to recall what
Was so important to
Say to you, "No, no, no"
I might have feared what
Would have changed two worlds

Perhaps I was wrong in
The crazy idea that
Being in the old churchyard
Would have lent an air
Of eternal truth to
What I had to say and
You might have taken me
Seriously for once
When I said, "I love you"

RUMORS

Rumors are.....that
I love you and that you love me too
But at our ages, who would ever
Believe a tale like that?

Tonight, I celebrate
Our laughter in all the yesteryears
And with this thin glass of white wine I
Toast especially that night we laughed
So heartily after everyone else
Had gone to bed and how we tried so hard
Not to awaken them!

And you remember when we were alone
How we fell upon each other and
Bubbled over into the night, quite
Overwhelmed with the joy of living!
Chablis or champagne...? I don't recall
The only thing that is clear tonight
Is that I *Loved!*

THE TRANSIENT LOVER

He had often dreamed of the
Artist he had once encountered
Whose harp rang out in resonance,
A flaring flow of melody,
Entrancing all who dared to love.

The vagabond retraced these sounds
A hundred thousand times or more,
Swaying harmoniously through
The hills and valleys of his dreams,
Tramping the marshlands and the dunes
To reach the shores of all the seas
And find re-entry to the source.

And after a long while, when these
Many colors had blinded his
Senses, he'd search by the faint sounds
Made by the winds brushing the reeds
While strings of violins shredded
What was left of a willing heart
Until his mind was split between
Reality and fantasy.

He could not stop this searching for
The lover in his dreams.....walking
Deserted beaches of the world
He'd find himself heaved upward—caught
Inside gigantic thrusts of an
Ever-surging sensual sea
Then floated downward to the thrills
Of open arms and mouth and breasts—
Seeking the handholds she only
Could provide that would satisfy
His lusty seaborn soul racing
To quickening fire consumed in

Waves of light brighter than any
Startling his younger days—then just
As suddenly—awakening
And wondering if it was but
Another dream.....until he slept
Again to chase the dreamgirl down
The closing cobwebs of his mind
And seek the notes that kept him bound.

I CANNOT SAY A WORD

I cannot say a word
But here is my heart
You know my heart well
And you can do as
You wish with...my heart
And I will never say a word.

If I had twenty years again
I would tell you more and more
Of the things in this heart
But I will never have
Twenty years again, and
I cannot say a word.

I will disappear
In the Great Silence, and
I will not say a word
But here is my heart
And you can keep it
Or, if you wish,
You can throw it away.

ALWAYS

The picture of you is always with me
And always my thoughts are of you;
The questions that I ask myself
Are never answered
Yet I wanted you to know that
I love you.
My thoughts, my heart, my soul
Are eternally with you!
And the rest?
The rest of whatever there is to my life
Can go to hell!

POEM ON BLUE

Just off the drawing board
This poem I send to you
So you can see just how it is
To make a poem on blue.

O' don't worry about the content,
No one loves anyone anymore;
Just something I thought up
When I was tired and thinking of you:

"I Love You!" poem on blue.

OH, LOVER!

Pull down my heart,
Hang up my hat,
Turn down the lamp,
Put out the cat!

IF WHEN

If when.....
If when, at times,
I have felt cheated
    by what I thought
    ought to have been mine,
    ought to have been loyal,
Then...on
The other hand,
I have been moved
    at how ample
    was the recompense
    of another that could
    never have been mine,
Yet, one who had the time to give
And gave, and was
.... loyal.

SUMMER'S JADE

It was the jade in her wild eyes
Hinting of other mysteries
That bade me follow helplessly;
And with that look, spellbound I came
Beyond the sound of rumbling hearts
That rushed and went their separate ways
Like hoofbeats of stampeding bands
Receding from a conquest land
Until they came and went no more.

The love I sing was for the first
Devoted and sweet chastity
In faces of adversity;
Laying on her blissful bosom
I knew then no greater vision
Would ever beautify my path
For she could touch the highest star—
Her lines were filtering and fine
The work of a long-studied art.

This mark of a once-gilded age
Still held profligacy of mind—
A crude, entrancing, uncut jewel
Left to show perpetual youth,
And the glint in her eastern eye
Revealed the far-off land to me
That I should hold and love with her,
To stay until the end of life
Or pay the consequence divine.

For she had power over men
Enough to carry me away
Or sail my soul to hell—and yet
What I feared was her departure,

That on some early morning's wing
I too would face the rising sun
And choose the west or want her ways
And disappear into the east
To find the greenery of peace.

Down narrow, twisting streets of time
I shouted to all passers-by, "This
Iridescent summer's jade is mine!"
Too soon I lost her in the crowd
Forced back when silence grew too loud
And love, this dream container thing
Became a play before it fled
With one last line, one common thread
The jade would gleam through my forehead.

TO MY GODDESS OF GARDENS AND SPRING

To one whom I will never forget—
An angel to me, literally
All overpowering—but not for
This alone, but for the lovely
Silken corridors of her exquisite
Mind and these revealed through her smile, the
Twinkle of her eyes, her graceful poise
A venus complete—standing among
The ruins of a stricken world
Venus of Milo
So lovely, so pure
Goddess of gardens and spring
Woman of grace and beauty.

CINDY'S LESSON FOR TODAY

Cindy, I'd like to have a talk with you
Concerning the matter of your dangerous eyes
For I fear they have *the power* and that
Some day, they may drive a man to kill.
Cindy, this is your lesson for today.

First, they're far too large; they absorb too much
Of the imagination. The dark irises
Expand and contract in such a way that
Squeeze one's soul out of existence and
Force it into a life-death struggle.
Cindy, this is your lesson for today.

Second, they're far too dark; they eclipse the
Revelled edges of your thoughts and one unable
To sense your responses clearly may crush
His lover to him with a hurt that kills.
I must tell you that your lover will
Not let you go without a struggle.
Cindy, this is your lesson for today.

I cannot advise you further, Cindy
Just take your lesson seriously, please, for your
Reactions may indeed determine
Who will live and who will die one day.

There is a kind of price that must be paid
By those who are of such beauty made.

THIS IS MILLIE FROM MILAN

Until then, he'd never touched a flower,
Never caught its breath sweetening his land,
Never felt this much softness in his hand,
Never seen all that God had made of man.

Until then, he'd never dreamt that it was
Possible for men to have a friend who
Asked nothing more than just to be a friend.
> *This is Millie from Milan,*
> *She is a friend of mine.*

The colors ran deep and rich through his face
While all the imagery passed of what
Life on this earth could hold for him clashed and
Choked his blood down through an eternity.
> Again, I said to him:
> *This is Millie from Milan,*
> *She is a friend of mine.*

He stepped forward, faltered, didn't speak, though
He tried to move his tongue, and then his hand;
Still, he just stood there in a kind of void.
Somehow, the two hands touched and melted,
The one a Viking spirit's, the other
> A soft lady's from Milan.

And for him to know more of God's work of man
He swore he'd look no further than in the hand
> Of sweet Millie from Milan.

D'ELLEN, GOD'S MAGNIFICENCE

The brush of her youthful soul wipes away
The years and time stands still upon this hill.
The press of her small hand, a jewel in mine
Reproduces strengths a thousandfold,
And God's loyal subjects stand trembling for
That which they behold, His magnificence.

While comparisons of people I have known
Flash bitter-bright kaleidoscopes on the
Backscreens of these tired Nordic orbs,
Hot liquid pools stronger than bonded steel
Solidify the moment when her gaze
Returns a misty quest for knowledge that
Lies beyond the reaches of us both, yet
It stirs an endless depth of hope and then
The imagination can't keep pace with
The faith it heaps splendidly at my door:
>Ah! I shall sleep
>Ah! I shall sleep
>My soul shall rest
>From dreams it had
>Envied others—
>Until she woke,
Walked part-way down this dusty road with me,
And did not fear my bulk and ugliness.

WEDNESDAY LOVE

Wednesday, the sky was blue
Thursday, I thought of you
Friday, school was out
I love you beyond a doubt!

ORIENTAL BUTTERFLY

Painted circles spotted
   yellow, blue and red
Flutter 'round my swimming head
   dust my bed
A flower of incandescent fire
   her taste inherited
   her touch softer than the wind
Her smile more pleasing than
   a thousand summer nights
This oriental butterfly.

                Silent thoughts of
                Little Patty Bartee

ORANGE CRUSH

That I did love her there can be little doubt,
Thus my confession to an unrequited love.
But we were mere children then, chubby and flush
Of cheek was she, bashful and shy was I.

Time changed all that; we lost each other in the
Years that came between, lost what love did mean;
In our metamorphosis, she grew her way, I grew mine;
But we held each other in our minds.

Dreaming tonight, I held her inside the moon;
Together we claimed an ancient love, savoring
A taste of youth, a full-blown piquancy—but age
Had mellowed us; all meant more and less.

Around her waist she wore a silkened sash,
Emblazoned with an *O-R-A-N-G-E C-R-U-S-H*.

PRETTY MARY

I called her Pretty Mary.
She was everything
She pretended not to be
For it cost her dearly
Compared to others her own age.
She often stood alone
Trying not to be, but
She struck such a contrast
That girls avoided her while
Boys, like bees, sought honey.
Tom Handsome was the first
To offer friendship, and
Now she receives her mail as
Mrs. Mary Pretty Handsome.
What's in a name, loss or gain?

MYRA BURCHETT

The dark-eyed child,
    last in a family of fourteen,
Has eyes that drive wedges
    into the foundation of a crumbling society.
Says she, "I only want to have friends and be loved."
    Says I, "That's not asking too much!"
Says she likes where she lives
    and the church where she goes,
Likes to sing in the choir
    and the people she knows.
Says I, "That's not asking too much
    for one who has eyes
    that drive wedges to brace
    into the foundation of a crumbling society!"

RAINING
WET THOUGHTS
ON MY PILLOW

I quit dreaming a long time ago;
They don't come true for me anymore.
Reality is my only task master;
I am toughened to its blows.

I'm the native who threw away
The pearl richer than all his tribe.

And if I seem saddened by the
Profile I have drawn of myself, it is
Because I have become weary of
Raining wet thoughts on my pillow.

SHOULD WE BUT PASS

Should we but pass along this road
Should you but pause to say hello
I would fall upon the ground and
Kiss it hallowed miles around.....
Should you pass this way again
You would find me here, my friend.

More of this love I shall not say
Words are too fragile to convey
All that our minds can best replay
For words once spoken slip away.....
Like half a lifetime from today
Since we passed here, yesterday.

THE LADY NONDESCRIPT

Vagaries of the mind pass as a part of living
And become neither great nor small in perception;
Averages, measurements, weights and balances
Lie bland within the grey mass while magnificent
Images of the Lady Nondescript play on
But never quite succeed in imprinting the mind;
It's just that one sometimes has a way of recalling
Certain aspects of averages, like the
Color of hair when it takes a definite turn.

Reminding him that men had loved her—from Scully
Square to all the war-torn cities of Europe, he
Saw half-shadows of the pair that had once clung so
Desperately in the corners of every
Dark evening across the world's wide back, while she
Denying neither friend nor enemy, served in an
Essential way, this woman of averages, to
Bind the broken, bleeding world together again.

What made her remembered most was not so much the
Half pleasure-joys and lusts of flesh she could conjure
As were the pictures on her dressing table, the
Pictures of her friends, her family, her children
That made her quite human; not to be neglected
Was the crucifix above her bed which seemed to
Remind the stranger that total ownership of
Anything earthly was not quite possible, that
All possession was a temporary stronghold
Which the dimming dusk would take away, and that man's
Own being was fading further into each night
And the only moments he could savor were those
That he could afford to pay for; nothing was free.

And on the streets by day, he saw her image in
A hundred faces that came his way but, alas,

The features sought were all too vague, coming from a
Memory born in human sweat, flesh-mixing in
"Off-limit" places; each time he'd try to recall
Her more distinctly to find her a second time...
Perhaps that wasn't her, but if it was, she too
Must have had misgivings in placing a face, in
Claiming one among many that had passed her way;
Yet, she had never lost her composure, she had
Never answered, never smiled, never acknowledged
The night before by day to any face that turned
Her way and it was only by night that one could
Find this Lady Nondescript, in darkened upper
Rooms, the pedestals of all forbidden places.

Later he would reason that as all faces are universally
Round to an artist, all women have full breasts and are
Beautiful to a stranger in a foreign land.

PAST THE MIDDLING HOUR

Only seconds ago
The hour was mine,
Our glasses were filled
With the sweetness of wine.

The glasses are empty now
Our hurried spoken dreams
Have fled, and you are gone.
It's well past the middling hour.

June 1964

TO EMILY BRONTE 1818—1848

Emily, you too were loved so deeply
By a strange kind of brutal love-making
Which I the beast Heathcliff did not have the
Power to understand in my heart in
This short life; to love was always to hurt.

How can one hold a flower without it
Bruising mightily? Why must the flower
Always fold inward once it has been picked?
Why can't one steal a kiss without regret?
O' it hurts to live and it hurts to die
And we were so caught up between the two!

I knew you once as Cathy
In a world we left so far behind.....
Still, just down the road to the Crossroads Grange
I see our initials carved into the
Old guide post pointing toward Wuthering Heights.

O' what Wuthering Heights there could have been
But time and a gypsy-like heart put an
End to joy in the flatness of living.

I WILL FORGET SOMEHOW

Somehow I will forget
The perfection I found there;
I will forget, somehow.
I'll say her dark eyes never
Made me wince, or that I
Could not stay in her presence
Without loving her, so
I left her and went away
To cry alone and wonder
If she ever cries for me.

In the long dark nights I will
Lie awake and dream of her—
In anguish, I will hold her
From afar.....if I drouse off,
I shall die, but then
I will forget her.....
Say, "I loved her
     deeper than my wounds."
Say, "I would choose her love
     here and now to any
     kind of life hereafter."
Say, "I loved her here in this world."
Tell her..."She never knew how much!"

Cloudlines

"To the high speed of ships that skimmed on cool silken paths, fluorescently lit like the Great Northern Sky, making these travels the happiest days of our lives..."

EASTER ISLAND MORNING

In the lonely hours of morning
I sailed away to Easter Island...
Now I live on a pretty green slope
In a seagrass hut overlooking
A peaceful blue lagoon beneath
Unnaturally picturesque mountains.

A fair maid, Leaia, brings me some
Taro root and tree-sweet papaya.
On Saturday, after I have slept
I may go fishing, or I may not.

AKU-AKU, the guardian eye
Spirit of the island world watches
To protect my private paradise.

Easter Island Sunday
24 September 1967

FAREWELL TO ROCK LAKE

I come to bid thee fond farewell
O' silent lake upon the hill,
You have my wealth of pennies and
All my wishes for good fortune—
Now I toss myself to chance for
School is out and you are losing
A sailor to a darker sea;
Too often this has been my chore
To wish a while, then close the door,
Yet, I'd rather be such a sailor
Sailing a deeper, freer sea.

Quietly, the sunset splashes
Its purple mark above the lake
And darker shades upon the deep,
And with each evening wave that breaks,
My face breaks with it; still, I ask
You "bid me well" as I go down
Immersed in hope, encased in dreams...
Just bid me to come up again!
For, I'd rather be such a sailor
Sailing a deeper, freer sea.

A castaway, venturing here like
The barnacle, the pilot fish,
Seeking something to hold onto—
I stand alone and stare into
Your mesmerizing arms, wondering
Aloud, where my course will lead me,
And anxiously await the news—
(O' I've learned the system well!)
As each clear thought flashes forth, then
Hesitates ...What ship? What ocean?
What Fiddler's Green?...and vanishes;
Still, I intend to be the sailor

Farewell to Rock Lake

Who sails a deeper, freer sea.

Cheers to the lake upon the hill!
My last cup of grog to thee—and
My new shipmates under the sea,
To challenges and risks we'll take
To live or die, as it may be;
For, we'd rather be such new sailors
Sailing the deeper, freer seas.

> Graduation from the
> U. S. Submarine School,
> New London, Connecticut
> Fall, 1956

HOME IS A PAST AND FUTURE TENSE

Anxiously awaiting—separation from
The seas of World War II, the young still whole
Stood in stateside naval air stations and
Cursed the Navy out in hot torpedo
Passion because it couldn't get us home
Fast enough to play the happy part of
War—for we just knew that there would be so
Many open arms expecting heroes
To walk right into them and never leave!

The heated atmosphere in Jacksonville
Would have risen several more degrees
From any talk to stay aboard, and plans
For a career would have resulted in
Immediate and treasonous deep-sixing!
Yes, home was the accepted place to be

For everyone, forevermore.....
But, the Navy had been good to me; I'd
Traveled globally in the best of health
And was far better off financially.

Home was a sparsely acred mountain farm
Where only in the best of times had there
Ever been two horses—usually
We teamed our one with a neighbor's to do
The plowing, logging, and the heavy work;
But, there stooped this seaman, three days later,
Foaming fire and drained—just from raking hay.

Sweating excessively I recognized
Blood poisoning in the arm surrendered
To the last siege of clinic bayonets
Required as signature for my release;
Then when I had run the borrowed team of
Horses through a swarming hillside beehive,
The decision to return to sailing
Was quick in coming home to me; only
Three weeks had passed since I had stood, waiting
For orders, this time to get back inside.

And yard by yard, the line grew longer as
The sailors who had given up the name
Now sought it for their home identity;
Strange, how the young will change directions
Perhaps more quickly than they would with time;
Home is a past and future tense and
Seldom honored in the present mind.

> Jacksonville Naval Air Station and
> Norfolk Receiving Station
> July 1945

THE LAST MIRAGE

Blue water, sun and sky filled his world;
He heard the cries of gulls circling over
Windswept dunes...and the restlessness of
Waves breaking and falling on the shore,
This scene...no more.

The old shipwrecked sailor made his way
Clad in his frayed and faded dungarees,
The gold ring in his ear his sole possession;
Beard salty and white, lips broken and blue,
Swollen and bleeding still, with no strength to
Sound his echoes, he staggered through the dunes
...Upon life's stage.

Real as life stood one long in memory:
The years had flown since meeting on this spit,
And this time was no mirage—God couldn't
Play this sort of trick! Yet, there she stood with
The water in her hands...and if He could,
It would be in the higher latitudes
Where warm air rushes over icy seas.
No, it couldn't be a trick this time;
"I must be strong"...

It doesn't matter now just how it was,
The Dottie Browns, the waters, suns and skies,
The clouds or ships that go a-sailing by,
It doesn't matter anymore for all
The beaches, suns and Sundays and the terms
That loves run on—you've heard the terms before?
But then, who hasn't...the beard, the ear-ring
Were but island souvenirs; no, I'm not
Afraid that someone will want to love me.
...I want to be loved.

"Yes, all ships have sails; mine was a fine ship.
Yes, indeed, a beautiful flying ship!

Yes, I would like a drink of water
From the hill spring near old Groton town;
Yes, the sea air is salty today
And, yes, there have been storms and wrecks;
Yes, thank you, I will...ah...ah...ah...ah...
And, there were broken sticks...and sails all
Ripped and torn...and men swept overboard...
Lost on the sea.''

''There were things I would like to forget,
Things I should have done, wanted to do.
Yes, the years have flown and I know now
That I must not steer that course again.
Quartermaster! Quartermaster!
Hard to windward! Hard to windward!
Fair winds to you...
Not at all, child! Not at all...it was
That way. Smooth sailing to you! Indeed,
My Dottie Brown...''

''I must not founder upon this spit—
I must be strong—for this—old Harpoon...
Harrrrr...pppooooooo...nnnn...nn...''

Upon his knees he fell, grasping at the
Air and figure vanishing before him;
On his face he bottomed deep into the
Warm greedy sands of this uncharted sea;
In his hands he clutched only weeds, planted
By the seabirds a season ago.
Here the ancient mariner shipped;
Another wave broke on the shore
Guided by an unseen hand so
That the Crystal be not clouded,
That his love be not forgotten,
Be not disturbed by its absence,
Or, resurrected.

THE FULL MOON, THE WIND, THE LEAVES

Last night I listened to a steady wind
    tremble, shake, and tear
The tender leaves and saw them all
    stretched out before a full moon—
Held nimbly by the wind in flutter-flight,
    their fragile stems still
Glued in nature's bond to branches—
    reprieving their departures
Yet wrung so unnaturally into limp
    blankets floating
Obediently inside the strange pallor
    of the moonglow.

I saw them torn as I lay down in an
    unfamiliar place
Made so by my own thoughts and the
    strangeness of myself of late.
I had hurried home from mixing with
    the evils of the day
And looking out into the night, I saw
    myself, a leaf, held
Only by a meager stem still weak and
    tender from the spring.

The light of the moon became the whole
    universe containing
All the yet unseen powers, mysteries,
    and ancient glories;
The wind became the life force,
    buffeting unmercifully
Until it trained or redrew elements
    to its own design;
The leaves became the lives of men
    tormented, twisted, ripped by
Their creator, yielding to the
    mystic voices of the wind.

Extracting from one a mixture of the
    three, I knew this night
That all lives were as helpless as
    the leaves I saw kite-flying;
Their frayed and jagged silhouettes
    against the moon's bright bulk
Formed a most ominous and dreadful
    personage that deeply
Purged my heart and soundly shook the
    empty casements of my soul.

I closed my eyes yet was aware that
    time would pass and the whole
Universe would change: the hot summer
    nights would make their play and
Pass into autumn and the incessant winds
    would finally
Twist the stems of the leaves from their
    resting place upon the branch;
The leaves would fall and the rains
    would come and the snow would blow and
Lie upon the leaves; and the leaves
    would rot and add their souls to
The richness of the earth and reappear
    one sunny spring in
Some rarer form of glory—perhaps a
    flower, a sweet herb,
A great tree...Who can really say?
    God, make me a blade of grass!

The helpless leaves marched in their appeal
    in straight single columns and
Brought loud screeching sounds and
    bright flashing signals to my mind's eyes
Remembering yesterdays of sweet, tender
    loves and the dried

The Full Moon, the Wind, the Leaves

Falling tears stuck to all the weary,
    lonesome, and bitter years.
Drifting along, this time to sea,
    I matched the leaves with slim peaked
Battle pennants flapping in time to
    the rumbling vibrations
Of excessive speeds, swing-flying in
    sequence on taut slender
Halyards hailing some valiant dreadnought
    engaging in action.....

Voices on the sea:
"Battle Stations! Battle Stations! All Hands
    Man Your Battle Stations!"

Voice under the sea:
"Battle Surface Torpedo. Prepare for
    Surface Action!"

Voice on the sea:
The Captain orders: "Engage and Destroy
    the Enemy!"

Sailor:
"Whose enemy? I don't hate anyone!
    What am I doing here?"

Gun Crew Captain in the dark:
"If they come up, we'll blow the hell
    out of 'em! Ready Pointer,
    Ready Trainer, first loads, seconds,
    thirds, and standby...All Ready!"

Tennerif:
"Pass the ammunitions! 'Praise the Lord
    and pass the ammunition!'"

Richardson:
"Shut your goddamn mouth! Haney's going
   to be a preacher!"

Tennerif:
"To hell with Haney!"

Haney:
"Damn you! Don't say 'Praise the Lord
   and pass the ammunition' in
   the same breath! You're the devil!
   You even look like 'im! See your horns?"

Tennerif:
"That's just my curly hair; I'm from Spain!"

Haney:
"But look at me...I look like Jesus!"

Tennerif:
"The hell you do, Haney! You don't even
   know who he was or what he looked
   like and furthermore I can knock
   the hell out of you!"

Above their voices the Command:
"All Stations! Open Fire! Open Fire!
   All Guns! All Guns! Open Fire!
   Target to Starboard! Surface!"

Sounds of firing guns in the dark:
"Ratta-tat-ta-ta-Boom! A-tat-tat-Boom!
   Ratta-ta-ta-Boom! Crack! Boom!
   Boom! Boom! tat-Boom! Crack!
   Crackle-rattle-tat-ta-Boom! BOOM!!!"

The Full Moon, the Wind, the Leaves

Somewhere below the water's edge
   lightning strikes and thunder
Shakes the teeth, the ears, the
   flesh and soul of the Mighty Dreadnought!
Steam and smoke boil upward and ring
   the scene in mock camouflage.

A voice rings out:
"All Stations Cease Fire! Cease Fire All
   Stations! Power Fire! Torpedo Hit
   Forward! Magazine and Engine Room!
   Flooding! Flooding!"

A voice in the dark:
"What happened to him?"

A second voice:
"The goddamn fool jumped from the bridge
   to the 0-1 level to fight the powder
   fire! Both his legs are crushed!
   Get a stretcher somebody! On the
   double! Oh my God, it's the Captain!"

*Clearly and from the spot of crumpled human
flesh on deck comes a quiet voice:*
"Get me a talker. Report conditions."

Talker:
"Power fire out of control. Ship flooding,
   five compartments, magazine and engine
   rooms forward. Three direct torpedo hits.
   Ship listing badly fifty degrees to port.
   Target faded from scope."

Violent explosions occur in the darkness
    "Whoom! Speew! Speew!!"
The world of water, sky and iron lights
    for a moment and
Silences the voices on the surface of
    the bubbling sea.

Voices come again from under the sea:
"Are the wounded below?"
    "Yes, all below!"
"Any serious damage?"
    "Only slight superstructure damage
    that we can tell."
"Then set the Cruising Watch. Normal
    Steaming! Soup down! Soup and
    crackers for all stations!"

Voices cease, drowned by hums of powerful
    electric motors and
Swishes of giant hydraulic rams, while
    churning swirls of a
Fluorescent sea leave nothing more
    than ripples on the surface...

And from the vastness of the darkened
    waste, I wakened to note
There were no changes in the moon, the
    wind, the leaves...and so I
Closed my eyes and followed myself down
    a quaint and friendly street
Into a world where care was no more and
    no more was no care...
The incessant winds blew on and I knew
    not when they ceased.

incident from yesterday's islands

in the morning...then,
he was a young sailor sailing the distant seas with
islands scattered, where he had a very close friend,
one he'd sought and found; there were mystic
things about his friend he'd never understood,
but long ago he'd learned the art of never asking
questions; so after his ship had docked, he'd made
his way to her humble dwelling, two rooms near
the shore where fisherfolk habit, and where
life-only necessities guarantee a plain existence;
his ship was sailing on the morrow, he'd not see her
again; they'd remained awake for hours talking of
the simple life, of her interests and of his, but
nothing ever seriously because they both were of a
dissipated sea race; he'd be on his way tomorrow
across the world, searching, searching, searching...

in the morning...now,
he hears her gentle voice sleep-murmuring in the
sea dawn hour; his eyes hold her forever fresh unto
his mind; then, in the vapor of new daylight, he
sees all there was for him to see—dark eyes, dark
hair, fair flesh—all there; and reaching out to touch
her just once more, his forearm strikes an object
alive and moving—he turns to look, and there
beside him lies a stranger, breathing easy, peaceful
and smile-dreaming; he looks to his friend for some
answers to his rasping-gasping questions; her sole
response comes without any surprise or hesitation,
"that's my husband," she'll not discuss the matter
further and sees him to the quai; shaken from the
strange experience and from the unanswered
questions that sting his mind, he thought he'd
understood all human race relationships, but
this must be the one yet undefined.

in the morning...*later,*
his ship sails; he never sees her again, yet he
ponders that strange encounter to this day; he
dreams about it frequently; each time, he wakes
himself—laughing out loud in raw disbelief; it
always is the same—in his dream she follows him
down to his ship with her gentle warm embraces,
her melting kisses that take his soul away from all
he knows, and he sails away—never satisfied with
the dream ending, for always there is the
"smiling stranger" sleeping peacefully right there
beside him; then when he sees him, he says to
himself over and over: "it's all a wild dream; it
never happened, and yet i have this innate feeling
that there is something far more gentle in our
human nature than we know, something we have
lost in the past, something we will never let
ourselves believe in—it is too simple for us to find,
we'd be inclined to overlook it if we found it;
life in the world that i was born into just cannot
be this simple—no, go away and stay away—it
simply did not happen"...still, he tries the
concept: "how far must we each travel to find
such peace of mind, my 'smiling stranger?'"

in the evening...*then,*
he wills himself from all such thought, such gross
simplistic folly: "it was a dream, it is untrue, it
never really happened...and never will again"
he cannot redeem his greatest fear that he will
perish laughing in fits that he cannot control; the
idea is his fatal flaw, yet he is ever laughing, all the
way into the grave, screaming out hysterically:
"what fools we've been, what fools we are;
we've missed the whole point of the story, the
whole damn point of living! hah-ha-ha-ha-ha-ha..."

incident from yesterday's islands

in the evening...ever,
his ship sails on, his dream continues.....
the dreamer is lost in his own dreamprints,
like the dancer chasing his own dancesteps,
atop all world reality, beyond the fringe of marking time.

THE LABORING WORLD
MAKES GOOD NEIGHBORS

I have sailed with men of all races
    in all places on earth
I have toiled beside farmers
    in good seasons and bad
I have labored with workers
    in factories where
The assembly lines keep rolling
    in life and in death
I have lived with strong men
    of varied persuasions
I have sojourned with Arabs
    in hot camel sands
I have enjoyed the customs
    in Oriental lands
And I have loved them all;
The laboring world makes good
    neighbors and friends
And I have loved them all.

SAILOR ON WATCH

It was a sunny day, many years ago
In a place far away from my native land;
The ship was at anchor off a windy spit,
Swinging to and fro in a churning searoad.
The wind in my hair, the sun on my bare back,
I soon tired of just taking the bearings
To keep the dreadnought from slipping her berth.
Anchored too far to see or be seen without
The aid of binoculars, I'd brought out the
200 power to make things come closer.
The day was lazy, like a rope yarn Sunday...
As I edged the glasses over the coastline,
I seemed to be the only one alive...
Then suddenly I saw them—real live people
Without any clothes—they looked like young maidens
Out for a bath in the warm salt sea waters
I could see them clearly—it was no mirage!
Beautiful bodies swaying upward and downward
Heaved by the surf, riding the waves, heads toward shore.
I balanced the glasses and eased back into
The old man's command chair, deciding that
There was nothing unusual here, for we
Were afloat in a greek archipelago,
A land filled with legends of beauty and love.....
The war finally was over and we all were
So tired...school was out and Mama Anderson
Was rendering lye soap under the old
Poplar tree near the hill spring.....Sharply, the blow
Struck my shoulder! I surged to my feet as the
Captain said loudly but with stern amusement,
"Sailor, you can be shot for sleeping on watch."

BLUE VALLEY FLIGHTS

To sweep away the dust collected
    from a dreary day, the
Driver exchanged an earthbound engine
    for a higher one, and
The plane became a vacuum, sucking up
    the troubled mountaintops.
Coasting over clouds, the quietude
    returning, the pilot
Dipped into vanilla ice cream mounds
    and surfaced on the blue.

In the softly quickening twilight,
    the baseball players
Five thousand feet below looked
    strangely alien, unaware
A bird above was photographing
    movements into memory...
The Hillsville Airport got a haircut
    late this afternoon and
The mowers left a fresh impression
    for wings to carry home.

When white light-ening off the mountain
    edges moved the mauve into
A midnight blue and profiled everything
    off velvet blackness,
The stars came out and chose the spots
    to glow on in the darkness;
The other lights were set like diamonds
    into reasoned rows and
Squares and angles, the setters had ignored
    the bold artistic
Randomness posed overhead each night,
    except for following

The natural progressions snaking
    from the valley floors.

There is excitement and a peace of mind
    that comes each time from
Flying over what is known to man—
    the crazy quilts of
Forests, pastures, quarries and the
    twisted asphalt puzzles
Smooth out, somehow, while in the air,
    into a rightful rhythm—
The contradictions stay the same,
    the interpretations
Now accept the contrasts so that each
    landing makes the heart
More willing to take the boundaries
    of daily living.

Frost still on the air before the melting,
    scooting under clouds
And racing shadows over hills to
    the New River Valley,
The captain flew to work this morning
    (if you can call this work)...
O' for more wings in later lifetimes
    and the privilege of flight!

TO FLY THE IMPOSSIBLE SKY

To fly the impossible sky is to
Fly when every possible cloud there
Can be appears—all at one time. This will

To Fly the Impossible Sky

Never happen, theoretically.
Yet, pilots will tell you that it does, though
The experience comes only to those
Who range afar and when the suspended
Envelope of fear gives way to sublime
Rays of sunshine, there will be no regrets.

On this immortal day, the mountains ranged
High to our left and to our right, their tops
Smothered in billowy masses so that
We could not tell their final destination.
Black and white cumuli grew through the dense
And low-hung overcast; ragged and dark
Stratus strings trailed toward the earth like liquid
Pearls dripping into a molten black sea.

Caught short before my goal appeared in sight,
We were forced upward into the misty night
On instruments to seek the footsteps to
Home base. Strange questioning and shadowy
Looks passed between my passengers on this
New vertical direction. The gas tanks
Held enough for a short detour, but it
Was the sightless search and unexpected
Rocks above us that kept us in the lurch.

With critical attitudes intended,
I dove for a thinner opening sensed
From some light outside...a century of
Faith erupted when a hundred thousand
Lights glowed up at us—beckoning us home!
Cheers broke out as we glided in and saw
That we had beaten the dark side of the
Mountain and flown an improbable dream.

LITTLE CLOUD IN BLUE

Silent as a kite
You drifted in and
   Out of my life
Playing tag with all
My wings could offer;
I'd grown accustomed
To your every move,
Making love to you.
The moments when you
Seemed to disappear,
   I begged a beg,
   "Don't leave me here!"
For I am lonely, too;
Stay in flight with me,
My little cloud in blue.

BEFORE OUR TIME

Old, they call us
Old before our time, they say
So proud of our achievements
Young, yet so gray.

One young sailor
Said, "Soon I'll have gray sideburns."
"Now why should you wish for that?"
A second asked.

"It's the latest," he replied
"Besides, the women like it!"

SKYCAB AT 10,000

"Out of 7,000, going to 10,000."
(Vernon's on the horn) *"Do you have our contact?"*
"172 in pattern..."
"Do you think you'll have enough clearance?"
"No factor here! Boy, it's looking better all
    the time—I can see Myrtle Beach already,"
    I can see forever—what a view to heaven!"
"Do you see the waves breaking on the shore?"
"Why sure, I can see the waves breaking on shore!"
"Are you at 10,000 yet?"
"Another hundred and fifty feet to go.
    This is N7343A, level
    at 10,000 heading eastward".....I'll never
    see clearer or further than I have this day
    and what a beautiful sight it has been—the
    grandeur of the mountain ridges and the wide,
    wide valleys and the separating streambeds
    form magnificent impressions that should be
    recorded somewhere...but for today, these sights
    are overwhelming to a man aboard a
    platform floating through an eastern sky, looking
    over, peeking down, perking his spirit up and
    around on a clear winter's day—flying high!

IMMUTABLE NEW YORK

New York is New York and never changes;
The raw spectacular and the dolorous
Remnants of humanity breed facial
Expressions that cannot be washed away
In the morning to fool the world at noon.
  Hold On To Hand Rails.
  Do Not Rest Hats, Canes,
  Umbrellas on Hand Rails.
  Do Not Sit On The
  Escalator Steps!
Subway cars keep rolling, turning, bouncing,
Jerking, swaying, reading riders—all read
Something on a Sunday in New York while
Whistles shrill and shrieking check track-clackings
——a rumble of noise and the lights go out——
The lights come on and the passengers stay
Staring with profound eye-intensity;
Did they find more light inside the darkness?
Man makes his way from one unlit jungle
To another without time to convince
Himself which of them was brighter, without
Foresight to choose the one where he belongs;
New York is a fine collector of the
Indecisive seekers and the staunchest finders.

CONNECTICUT

Rocks, ponds, oaks, rushes,
Sparrows and yellowbreasts
Shake loose spring's silence in May
And cold trinkling brooks
Run away with the breeze
To mock man's advances
And keep him at bay
While the twenty-first
Century whips on its way
The past keeps renewing
Its pledges with Nature
So all shall be forced to remember!

SOUTHERN ROUTES

This is a world of moving people
Going somewhere all too fast
And I must not get caught up with them
For I do not seem to be
Heading in their direction yet;
I'll come along at some point,
Just don't rush me now...too many things
Along the way compete for
My attention and I prefer to
Take the time to pass the day,
To be polite and kind, to be more
Human, if I can, along
My southern roots, giving directions
Slow and well, especially
To the foreigner who does not
Understand the dialogue.
I don't mind you passing me by; but
I hate the thought that you would
Kill me on the way to church.

CHATEAU LUDE

Only the deep echoes of the french horns
    in the forest
And the jubilant sounding of trumpets from
    the high walls
Heralding comings and goings of
    hoofbeats and riders
Could decipher the scales of the human
    spirit and mind.....

Infused with the triumphant sounds and
    spectacular sights of the past,
The soul surges and leaps and keeps pace
    with the dazzling displays of rich
Violet-reds, amber-blue-greens, silvers and
    golds, and purest of whites
And calls forth the stars and a shimmering
    half moon from scheduled sky rounds
To reflect on the spirals of wet turns and
    sprays in beautiful forms
Unleashing new music from vibrant harp
    strings that pluck-pulse each synapse
Of the imagination to be wondrously,
    joyously tripped.

Sounds muffle, then fade, to a tone of past
    silence, as the
Single, last torch darkens the mind scenes
    to antiquity.....
And,
    one finds himself back in the
    twentieth century.

Experiencing the Son et Lumière Historical Pageant
on the Loir River   Lude, France   6 July 1984

QUAND JE PENSE À TOI

Je marche dans la rue de Fleurus
Et quelquefois je pleure, pour toi,
Quand je pense à toi,
Quand je pense à toi.

Je marche dans la rue de Fleurus
Je vois les murs, les trottoirs gris
Et quand je lève les yeux
Le ciel et les nuages sont aussi gris et sombres;
Puis, quelquefois, je pleure pour toi
Dans la rue de Fleurus.

Mais quand je pense à toi...
Oh! mais quand je pense à toi,
Les murs et les trottoirs sont roses
Le ciel et les nuages sont bleus et blancs
Et puis je ne pleure plus
Car tout est bien (je souris)
Dans la rue de Fleurus.

Paris, 1977

WHEN I THINK OF YOU

I walk in the street of Fleurus
And sometimes I cry, for you,
When I think of you,
When I think of you.

I walk in the street of Fleurus
I see the walls, the sidewalks grey
And when I raise my eyes
The sky and the clouds are also grey and somber;
Then, sometimes, I cry for you
In the street of Fleurus.

But when I think of you...
Oh! but when I think of you,
The walls and the sidewalks are rose
The sky and the clouds are blue and white
And then I don't cry anymore
For all is well (I smile)
In the street of Fleurus.

Paris, 1977

THE WHISPERING WINDS OF QUEBEC

The whispering winds of Quebec
Tell me a story and I know
That it's true—of the rivers,
The woodlands, the flowers, and you.

I watch the world in gasping awe
(O' please my joyful heart be still!)
While the evening sun crys to stay
Then, sadly slips behind a hill,
Its tears dried in a reddened sky
By the whispering winds of Life
Promising new tomorrows as
Fresh and as bright as the chilling
Of frost and the sparkle of light.

Caught in its spell, daydreaming, on
The churning waters of St. Lawrence
Rough-riding the eroded cliffs
Of some forgotten time—I watch
The dreams and lives of men flow past
And pour myself into their cast—
Feeling my waistcoat stain with blood,
My body twist and sprawl inside
The murky, muddy, wasted mire—
And find I cannot move or hide.

Through the mists of newborn morning,
The sun's strong rays filtering down,
I feel the value of my wounds,
My traded blood comes home to gruel;
The veil of smoke begins to rise,
The wild screams cease to quiet-quilt
The war-torn Plains of Abraham.
All who fought here took something home;

There are no losers tucked inside
These fields of dark rich earth patterned by
Flowers of blue and wooded hills
Enriching countryside and you.

Your arms about me, soft and sweet
Your glowing fires that warm my feet
Where love lies heavy, dreaming light
And pale peach blossoms bloom at night—
You are the silver glintings of
Your tall church spires aimed to protect,
You are your soldier's courage and
The victory they won, Quebec.

> First Visit to Quebec
> 4th of July 1960

JE ME SOUVIENS

Here, the bluffs, the hills, the spires and sky
Attempt to reach the height and hopes of man
And span the reaches of desire through
Swift and churning waters of emotion.
Here, embedded in a cast of gold,
The sun sets red so when the humblest
Dreams are shattered in the pale and gloom
Of evening, they are not entirely lost.
Though cold gray mist may in deep shadows stay,
The robins will perch and continue to
Sing on a theme well-known, so bright and gay
That you will listen and forget what was.

> Quebec, 1960

APPALACHIA, APPALACHIA
WHAT WILL FUTURE GENERATIONS SAY?

The ability of a people to dream
Is manifested in the structures and the
Art forms they leave to God and man and little
Else in their contributions depicts so well
The character, the genius, and splendor
Of a race; their ruins bear witness through the
Ages to help all those who follow design
Their brand of culture, nation, aspirations
And lend a measuring stick for progress made
Toward the proof that "Art is long and life is short."

Ancient Egyptians, Chinese, and Romans
Display what greatness is in its best forms;
By circumstance, all civilizations pass,
So then England and France are but brave children
Full of imagination and energy
Limited solely by the boundaries of
Sea and land; still they dream while Russia keeps
Future-building, hoping its people will not
Lose the dream; there are as many architects
As there are nationalities—but only
One dream and it is the same for all mankind.

The grand cathedrals of the Middle Ages
Star-point to God with strength and vision few of
Today's inhabitants can comprehend, while
Marble structures of the Greeks mock the power to
Imagine of Twentieth Century man.
Had we but claimed our inheritance to dream,
We could look around and see much more than the
Accepted need for a great war machine; we'd
See and hear the sounds of progress being made—
Our aspirations under construction.

Instead, we choose to hear lipped philosophies
And sit watching while our land declines through its
Institutions: corrupt ministers serve in
Every standing temple—moneychangers, all!

To identify with greatness, we will pay
Large sums to visit Cairo, Rome, and Athens.
Who will make their way to Appalachia
Five thousand years from now? What would they find?
Might there be a standing testament of time of
Our ability to dream? America
Is but an infant; Appalachia was
Just conceived—with all the opportunities
For childhood play and the memories of sleep.

Appalachia, O' Appalachia!
Shall we choose to dream and live eternally?
Or, blow away as dust in the winds of time?

Relearning Knots

"To learn more about the world we'd sailed over, all
the great ports and nations and peoples we'd seen..."

A RECKLESS WIND

There is a reckless wind that blows
That swallows trees from shifting rows
And carves its name in drifting sand
To seize upon the truths that stand.

It buffets heads in sun and rain
It burns them red, then dries the brain
Shouting long its sermon and song
Preaching in new philosophies.

By what measures are these made true?
The night sits in the dimness, too.
Can wrong bring forth a thing that's good?
In what proportions, if it could?

If wrong can be a discipline,
What limits such a reckless wind?

QUERY TO THE SEA

To the white restless foam about me
To the blue silent depths below me
There is some urgent thing calling
Something I must surely know—oh,
I wish that you could tell me more
First, you whisper, then you roar!
Now, tell me once again
Where does the soul begin?
And from your murmur low
Where did you say it ends?

AND HE LOOKED DOWN AT MOSES

And He looked down at Moses and explained,
"You are not what you think you think you are
But you are really what you think you are,"
And Moses with his two black soulful eyes
Looked up at God, sheepishly, and grinned.

Reed slim Moses fished off the submarine
Trying to catch the frisky scales grazing
In the tank moss; we'd always hear the splash
As he forgot the roundness of the ship.
One night the mighty cook took some offense
To what was said returning from shore leave,
"I'll hit you right between the running lights!"
And flattened him against the conning tower;
The Captain stole a secret from the Universe,
"When you think you are supposed to handle
All the situations handed to you,
You must reach inside your heart and venture
Out for fish you were designed to capture."

                    Anchored Off Southern France
                    1959

THE LITTLE SOLDIER

A basket on his head for a helmet
And an old tin pan for a drum,
He pretended he was a soldier with
His marching and his little wooden gun.

The sunlight shown in his face even
In the shade as he marched and shouted
To rout the enemy brigade and
A confident look with every little
Smile revealed his great success.

On and on he marched with every
Imagination before he stopped to rest.
I questioned his purpose and wondered
If he knew just what he had begun
Keeping step to the beat of his drum.

Helmets, drums, and guns
Helmets, Drums, and Guns
HELMETS, DRUMS, AND GUNS
Are the universal enemies
Of all the children I know!

OUTSIDE OF SCHOOL

I know I should have gone to school today
But singing birds and flowers kept me away
And we had to do what we'd said we'd do,
There's not many understands our kind, Sport
Especially teachers and the older folks,
But if they sat by this window and could
See all the things I see, they'd all agree.....
There's that flying squirrel that leaps off the

Schoolhouse roof every day about this time,
They're the queerest little creatures...and there's
Red-headed Woodpecker who lives inside
That big old chestnut tree...why, there's all kinds of
Other birds the likes of which you've never seen
Blues, yellows, reds and rainbows once I thought—
You saw it, too? ...yes, I must confess, it's
The outside of the schoolhouse I like best;
Of course, you don't have to worry about
Anyone because you belong to me
And I do all the worrying for you...
Come on, Sport, let's go before somebody
Sees us here and connects us with that old
Schoolhouse there...it's just you and me and it
Looks all clear up ahead, so we'll take the
Hollow along the branch to the top of
The ridge where we can see anyone that
Comes a-lookin' for us...maybe one day
When it's not so busy there, we'll come back
And go inside and take our seats and talk
To the teacher just as if she were there;
We'll tell her how deeply we feel—how much
We do appreciate what she's doing
And just because we don't plan to stay today,
Is not that we're unmindful—it's just
That we have got so much to do, right Sport?

> Apples to two wonderful
> Schoolteachers at Nick's Creek,
> Miss Margaret White and
> Miss Grey Buchanan,
> who gave the greater love that
> others might understand and have;
> their voices still ring in the
> lives of all they touched.

AND I LAY DOWN

And I lay down in
The old country road
And wallow in the
Dirt and laugh until
It hurts and look up
At the clear blue sky!
O', there was a time
I had time for such
Antics—it's a fine
Way to really get
Your belly laughs out
Rolling, wallowing
In an old country
Road because you feel
So good about life!
And you don't have to
Worry, no one will
Be coming along...
And when they do
They'll only see where
Something has been making
Funny stripe marks
In the soft dust and
Though they may wonder
They will never know
That there could be
Such Happiness
Experienced
Here on earth.

EDUCATION BEYOND ALL ARGUMENTS
From the Children of Speedwell Elementary School

These scraps of drawing paper....an art of
Glued-together rags of red and green
Left on my lap, stuffed down my back, with
Just a sheen of yellow flowing past,
Paying me in green and gold....so, this
One is for you, *"fome Becky and Judy."*

Greater than the worlds of greed mixed in
Country and city politics, and
Equal to a school man's arguments
Too sublime to be defined, or understood,
These changing colors hold the eyes transfixed
And wondering what's coming next!

These sheets of crayoned tablet....make art of
Stuck-together bits of orange and blue
Shoved on my lap, crammed down my back, with
Just the glow of amber gliding past,
Paying me in checks and jewels....so, take
This one and share it with the fools.

A Wythe County School Bus Driver
Spring, 1977

LEARNING TO LEARN

Growing up is difficult
Should be a birthday rule
Becoming something or
Someone you never knew,
Beholding what the charter
    winds have willed.

Learning to reach for wisdom
Should be one's stock in trade
Lighting the tapers in
Bolting the doors without,
Hearing *Love's Voice* answering
    unafraid.

WORD POWER

There were those who carried the Bible
With them wherever they went.
They could quote it verbatim;
You ask them and they had the answer.
They would get so excited and shake
The book with both hands above their heads
Declaring every word of it
To be the gospel truth
When it was common knowledge
That most could not read a word
From it or a sack of flour
Much less understand what they had read,
So great is the word power of God.

TO YOUR HEALTH — À VOTRE SANTÉ!

Be concerned about your health,
Both physical and mental;
Don't worry, just be concerned.
Spend your health wisely—for when
It's gone, there is no more.

TIME?

Time? Why time is nothing
You can see or taste or
Feel your finger on, for
It has no beginning
And no known ending; just
A thing like many things
Titled to be something.
It does not grow or age,
But all else changes in
Respect to it. Time is
A timeless abstract thing
That has forever been.

A LIFELESS LIFE

The epitaph on the tombstone read:

> Died at Thirty
> Buried at Seventy

I thought of someone I knew then and now.

CLIMBING TO COAST

When you see someone coasting
And you are envious of him
Remember
That somewhere along the line
He, too, had a hill to climb.

PERSISTENT LITTLE FLOWER

"It's just a little old flower with its head bent low
And will never amount to anything great we know,
For it didn't attend the recognized local high
And left our elementary a few credits shy."

People plainly told it that it couldn't if it would
Even though it kept on showing evidence it could,
And it no longer mattered if it ever got degrees
When it could go on doing well anything it pleased.

The letter came from the University one day:
The points were too short to fit their graduate bouquet;
Being so selective would assure all of the blooms
Only "tenable" positions in alumni rooms.

They closed by saying that it was sure it understood
And it showed it did with even greater adulthood—
Swinging, laughing, fiber sides pooched out more than it ought,
Why it'd already doctored more than "their" schools had taught!

It simply chose expansion into more Ph.D.'s
From vastly superior life universities
Saying what it had to say far more efficiently
Than could be said self-chained to "our" University.

LITTLE BOY, SOMEDAY
YOU TOO COULD BE AN ENGINEER

Little Boy,
This is the way that it is done:
    You sit here in the dirt,
    Pick up a pebble,
    Roll the red skate wheel
    Once with your left finger,
    Spit at the building,
    And throw the pebble
        down
            the
                street.
I don't know why it's done this way,
But it is...Little Boy, someday
You too could be an engineer!
But you must first learn to put things
In their proper order; it doesn't
Matter what you choose so long as you
Find some kind of order to put
Them in...for now, this will be fine:
    Pick up a pebble,
    Roll the red skate wheel
    Once with one left finger,
    Spit at the building,
    And throw the pebble
    Down the street...
        see,
          it
                works!
You can change the world
With your new machine,
Your order of operation,
And you may call it
    ...Revolution...

A boy absorbed in play
Lancaster, Pennsylvania July 1982

79

DOOR WAYS

Someone who has lived enough should
    give a course on doors
Paneling a lifetime study
    of past and future lores
The lecture series should include
    fact and observation
Yet go beyond the treatise of
    principled opinion
To tap imagination and
    the sensitivity
Of poetic postulation
    and mind discovery.

For doors are more than openings
    and closings of account
They stand up for all barriers
    of entry in or out
Their obvious utility
    comes sliding, swinging by
Held in close check by classic posts
    or saintly flying high
To hide, reveal, hold in, lock out
    animals and weather
Passengers and residents both
    singly and together.

Users are the common lot of
    world-wide populations
But are defined by what they're not
    through negative persuasions:
The angry aim to smash at life,
    the sad to close it off;
The derelict to pick the lock,
    the lost suppose it off.

Doors should be known intimately
    by their users letting
Designing come from self and
    societal goal-setting.

Door specialities perk up the
    palette mostly from supplies
Used by artisans and craftsmen
    in beautiful surprise
The grand cathedrals mold carvings
    centuries-in-making
Museums hinge thick bronzes with
    sculptured art painstaking
Warehouses and air terminals
    measure up to giraffes
Houses and horse barns cut their dutch
    doors in hole closing halves
Rooms can take them with or without
    cold locks of secrecy
While vehicles, ships and planes use
    hatch-like accuracy.

Yes, someone should teach a living
    course on our adeptness
In choosing doors or blindly
    offering our acceptance
How can we rectify the portals
    of the orphanage
And look another way at the space
    window for launched jets
Where are we when the doors of time
    are sealed by the dying
And what of the troubled who may
    soon give up on trying?

Door Ways

The uniqueness of the door comes
    in its final passage
From views of mortal ground to our
    most important vantage.
Preparation for this course may
    perplex all of mankind;
The most difficult to open are
    door ways of the mind.

> To the door ways of uniqueness
> opened by Henry Pickle and
> his coat of many colors

AN INDICTMENT

Voices of the Living
Voices of the Dead of Flanders Field

Cold winds sweep this winter land;
We lie beneath the icy sod of Flanders fields.
Spring is all but forgotten.
Ye so mistook the quarrel.
Ye caught not the torch!
Stars of youth no longer shine.
The poppies of Flanders fields ask, "Why?"
Tender leaves have gone to waste.
We lie as dust in many a far-off place.
Comrades we knew do not return...

Oh, ye too, Little Candles, so low doth burn.
We no longer hear songs of peace.
The din of battle blasts the low country.
Wars are still raging.
Ye broke the faith—mistook our quarrel.
We talk of forty thousand dead,
We sleep in Flanders fields!
As though even one poppie were not enough;
Forgive them, Father, for one poppie!
One is proud of his kill;
    He paints it on his tank, his shield
    Boasting, a man among men that can kill.
Ill health overtakes him otherwise.
God, how did we ever live, love, and kill?
    We so mistook the quarrel!
We found the wars we had fought a mistake!
    And all the governments that we had ever known,
    Had made such asses of so many fine men at home
    And now our comrades turn to clay.
We were drafted too young, and ye "wasted" us away!
    Father, forgive them for even one poppie!
And the hundreds of thousands of poppies
    That lie broken or dead,
    But sleep not in many a far-off Flanders field.
Ye cannot pose us again,
Our comrades do not return in the fall,
Like a family portrait, for another take.
    We sleep not in Flanders fields.
Oh, my God! How did we ever live, love and kill?
    We so mistook the quarrel!
We sleep not in Flanders fields.

Written after the Vietnam War

WE NEVER DID AGREE

In philosophy and act, we never did agree;
I was young and they understood all that
Too belligerent, headstrong, and wrong to change.
Their heads turned gray and their lovers died
And I grew a little in the mind;
They were more tender toward me and less
Stalwart in their own predetermined course,
I came down and they reached up it seemed;
My road was blinded by an unknown destination
And theirs was shaded by a slightly lifting fog.
We passed each other on the road yesterday
Traveling but by different directions;
We looked sadly at each other as we said hello
Crying inside for the things we'd never understood
Little doubting the other to push forward,
Showing respect for believing in and
Sticking to the life road each had chosen
—And I could tell you—if you would listen.

HIDDEN BEHIND HYPOCRISY

One may display his feelings
    at the supermarket
Another behind closed doors
    with his centricities
    hidden by a kind of
    Sunday hypocrisy.
I pass no judgment,
    I participate;
    yet, I'd choose to have
    the supermarket slate.

AND SOCIETY'S GREAT
TABOO WALL FELL DOWN

Ice on the mountaintop
We could go no further
Nor did we wish to
Sun
Silence
Cracking ice
The sky, blue silk
The ground, white lace
For the gold of her hair
And the pink of her face
Sudden clumping sounds outside
And society's great taboo wall
Came tumbling down
Taking a thousand other
Dogmatic barriers with it...
It would be a freer and far better
World in which we could live and love;
Few things short of an act of the eternal
Seemed fated: It would be
What we made it.

FRIENDSHIPS

Friendships you don't always choose;
Sometimes they blow in with the wind
Bringing someone you can't afford to lose,
One you might want to think of as a friend.

Don't make them too lasting. Don't get too close.
Don't ruin them. Save them. Temper them slow.
Love them. Don't say goodbye if you can choose.
Hold on to the point of contradiction.

THE MAN AND THE BIKE

During the Day.....
The man was pushing his bike fifteen miles
From town, pushing it up hill, riding it down,
Carrying his possessions on his back.
Perhaps he's been to the local market
And now he is returning home, who knows?
Maybe he's been Christmas shopping, for that's
The way it is when one is very poor,
Even in this land of plenty, this land
"Of milk and honey." Certainly, it's one
Thing to be rich and own a bike, and quite
Another to be poor and own one. Then,
There was the man who rode his bike for his
Health; the doctor had told him that if he
Ever stopped walking or riding his bike
He would never walk again, and so he
Rode his bike constantly for the rest of
His life.   It was a day in the third week
Of December, when no snow had fallen
But the temperature was very low.....

During the Evening.....
Weather was threatening, snow and dark came
Early, yet there was the same man—pushing
His bike along, heading out of town, dressed
In meager clothing and wearing a small
Grey pack on his back. It was uneasy
To look at him; two men who were watching
Said to each other: "Looks like he's movin'
On!" "Yeah, but it's hard on a man on a
Night like tonight, in this kind of weather,
This time of year—awfully cold!" The man
With the bike went on, and the two watchers
Stood watching. He didn't look back, but a

Third man looked at him, and he hurt deep from
Within, because he knew what it felt like
To be alone, on a cold wintry night
With no friends near, no warmth, and no mirth;
Nothing but dying and death all around.....
As you close your eyes and try to sleep just
For a minute, the terrible killing
Sounds of the howling winds whine and groan in
Your ears—you can't make them go away and
In some way, they seem to remind you of
The worst things you have ever heard or knew
About and these things keep coming back to
Drive you insane. Then you die a little
Inside and as the cold ice rain slips down
Under your clothing, you end up hating
Something, anything, and you feel equal
To an animal that can kill and rob
For something to go into its stomach.....
That's what it's like to be hungry; you don't
Care any more; laws mean nothing when it
Becomes a matter of stomach over
Mind. All moral codes slip by the wayside
When people are desperate.....The someone
Who was hurting inside, turned to invite
"The Man" home for the night, in from the
Cold; by then, "the man" already had faded
Into the shadows of the frozen night.

During the Night.....
He was a man like my grandfather found
Lying dead in the barn one wintry day
Long ago. He wore the face that many
Men wear, drawn, and dower from life's long trek.

The Man and the Bike

You have met "the man" before: you passed him
A hundred times along the roads, on trains,
At bus stops, in out-of-the-way places,
And in local markets buying canned beans.
Oh, you have met the man all right, but what
Bothers you most is that you have never
Seen him smile. His life has been too weary,
His trip has been too long; he had far too
Many troubles, too many things went too
Wrong, and there was not enough in his life,
Not nearly enough, to let him know that
Life is a pleasure to be lived and just
Enjoyed: there is no sense in trying to
Make it make some sense, for it can't be done.
This man has walked a beaten path; he knows
All there is to know yet, now, sometimes, still
There is no other place to go; so he
Hits the open road to cure these human
Maladies, things that are too sick in his
Soul. Offering him shelter on any
Given night would not say much to him; would
Not have brought him back; he knows too much of
Life...he's too far down the road to come back.
He chooses, then, to sleep beside the road
Where his agonized, pale, restless eyes search
Endlessly for sure cures of the soul. And
What he sees and hears tends to separate
Him from his earthly brothers. And those who
See and truly understand "the man" have
Strong desires to join him by the road sides
Of the world, cycling in their search for cures......

A PERSON OF OPINION

Her recognition was slight
Her spoken greeting barely audible
She had heard that I was a person of opinion
Pursuing some sort of wiser philosophy
I suppose; she had heard wrong
I was only the man who
Had known her father's sister and
The girl's mother with whom she now spoke,
Had known them too well
But then was I to blame when I
Was only twelve and she forty,
I was fourteen and she thirty-six?
There was some need to be satisfied
Somewhere among those jumbled ages and
It was this that I was still trying
To separate from the wearied philosophies of
You can't, you can, you shouldn't, you should.

Compounding it all, it gave me no fear
Of the past, the present, or the future
I found everything basic and human in it
Everything godly and ungodly
Depending on how you were versed
It had all amounted to nothing but life;
I had been the scientific observer
I, the unpolluted model for comparison
They, the creatures of experiment;
The hypothesis that people were only human
Had been proven correct once again, and
I was the true believer.

ONE WHO DARES
THE STEEPNESS OF THE SLOPE

Terra verte and ocher
Sliding into view
As Jack climbed up
The steeper slopes
And stopped to rest
Upon the crest
That suddenly caved in!

Jack screamed out loud
And grabbed at twigs
That split and broke
And clawed at all the
Avalanching earth
Running down into
The terrible soft slide
Barely managing
To stay alive!

Energy spent in
Great heaps of soil
Jack turned to ascend
The steepness of the hill
Topping the crest with
Great accomplishment
When the earth slid out
From under him again
He ran, he fell
He jumped, he yelled!

He knew not why he ran
To and from the slope
The fearful slide
The mongrel faces, too
And for awhile he felt

He had defeated all
The greater hordes
Of chasing mongrels
Who were afraid
To even attempt
The steepness of the slope.

In passing them
In his escape
Jack slapped them down,
Some fell beneath the slide
For they were jealous
Of his gain and pride
Yet there were scores
And little chance
Of escaping all;
Hunter and the hunting
Fought savagely
For what he knew was his
Jack vowed that none
Should take what was.

He won this bout and
Traveled with his own
Into a far
More peaceful land
Where in disguise
Centuries before
He had plied
The trade of shepherd;

Until darkness fell
And saved him from
This mongrel hell.

ON THE INFINITE
NATURE OF FRIENDSHIPS

To my door come letters from old friends
And I read them with a quick interest.
These are good friends from faraway places
Who still recall the moments that were shared,
Days of a colorful passing from time
We could afford to spend on each other.
A blue envelope lies on the table
Ripped open indiscriminately
In my haste to get to what was inside:
"Service and Industry USA 20¢"
I read, aimlessly, while lost among
The complexities of lines that criss-cross
The flavors of blue, red, and yellow
Flowing cold to warm from the artist's eyes,
Bringing different values into mine
On the infinite nature of friendships
And something that a friend revealed, simply
How so often we can see a thing of
Beauty in the ruins of a churchyard
Yet are unable to see anything
Alluring in the ruins of a man;
Holding the thought, I am lost as a leper
Hiding myself and my disease from
A world that shuns me for what I am—
I do not understand the society
Of my birth: Man is all, I conclude,
And nothing else matters or compares.

PEACE IN THE SETTING OF THE SUN

The sun setting before my eyes, I stayed
Standing for a long while without moving
Upon the summit of the mountain where
I could see far beyond the other hills;
The disc of orange and red flamed out to the
Night lights and I looked to them for answers
In the stillness of the dusk that followed
Thinking of the many suns and stars that
Had born witness to all things of this life
Into the depths of creation and I
Was reawakened to the grandiose
Nature and splendid beauty of the world
Yet frightened by its somber visage and
Terrible isolation—rejoicing
In the spirit of mankind trying to
Learn and understand such awesome factors.
I knew that if I couldn't ask such life-
Holding questions that there was nothing more
For anyone beyond what could be seen;
Pondering, it seemed the sun was the law
That pulled all things and the world on ahead...
It was in these long silent moments that
I felt most like an element of the
Universe—not indispensable, but
Like all others which come and go and this
Gave me a sense of value in my life—
I found the greater freedom that I sought
And the experience cost me nothing!

THE PLOW WILL SURVIVE

Get it all together
Then take it all apart
Invent a thousand machines
Attach their accessories
Do with them as you please and
When you have worked them to death
Only the plow will survive.

Past the last of the fervor
Laying computer tech lines
Bossing the factory hands
Tilling that new purchased ground
Reforming your own sacred
Group and forcing their values,
When all of your beautiful
And delicate robots have
Relinquished their roles to a
Billion others and they too
Are utterly extinquished
Blown to waste on the world-winds
Of mankind and untamed by time
The plow, alone, will survive.

Sift through civilizations
Of all different markings
Dumping the moralists, the
Love lusters, the pageantry
Followers, the voice dreamers
Those who would riot, pillage,
Rape and destroy and forget
All to make liars of those
Prophets of past history
When this has been done and more
The plow can only survive.

All the rich of the world who
Made it by prostituting

The lowly will continue
For slavery has worked so
Well with all the caste systems
Of the world and together
Ignorance and religion
Have been a successful team
Making it difficult to
Tell the one from the other
Regardless of allegiance,
And their education in the
Ivory tight echelons
Has only prolonged the last
Frontier of slavery to
Mere capitalism and
When this education fails
As it seems to be doing
The plow will justly survive.

When finally all of man's
Created kingdom shores are
Eroded by tides and the
Eating swells of the human sea
When all royalty and great
Pretenders to rightful claims
Have ceased to exist and
The bluebloods have been rinsed away
By torrents of rushing time
The plow, above all, will survive.

And the age-old prophecy
Shall be fulfilled:
The plow, the meek, the lowly
In heart and in soul shall rule
Amid even the dust and
The ruin of a doomsday clime
It will be all to survive.

AND LAUGHS AT ALL
YOU AND HEAVEN KNOWS

I'll not forget this setting star
Burning into all tomorrows,
I bathe myself in its fire and light
And read the proof I've found
On both sides of the slate, how
Alone, I found the artist, the
True sculptor of the human bust,
The smooth silk flowing of a mind.
Nature! Nature!
Generous of spirit
Joyous of heart
Hand thrusting torch
Above the darkest night
...and once, how this
Sicken son fell into the sea
Grew lost and weary of the way
Had reached for nature's flaming torch
That lighted jettys of the bay
Leading toward the Great Entreat
That soothes and cools a southward soul
And laughed at all that you and heaven knows.

AND ALL THE MONKS AGREED

Among the thistles growing there,
The old Benedictine
Chanced upon a golden flower
More delicate and fair
Than he'd found blooming anywhere
And then one day he lost it.

He searched the gardens of the land
And tramped the deserts down

He rambled over snowy caps
In quest of one to match
A flower, it seemed, that must grow
Only through heaven's floor.

He stayed with brethren in their stalls
High on craggy ledges
To learn the origin of bloom
And replicate its kind.
They said it must be very rare
Because in all their ancient scrolls
It wasn't listed there!

Descending past the cold, grey walls
Over jagged mountains
Holding up a falling sky
Giving solace one more try
For what he thought must surely grow,
He heard the quavering voice:

"Listen, Brother Benedictine,
The flower that you knew
Was never meant to be
For silver seeds are seldom sown
Among the thistles overgrown,
And golden ones will never smile
Between the thorns wild, but
There was one dropped a few springs back
Meeting these conditions
So you see, it might have been, yet
It could never really be.
That flower of gold purity
The one you thought you found
That healed your broken heart...
Too many thistles, too many thorns!"
And all the monks agreed.

La Brunante

"To all the tomorrows of times yet unlived,
in uncharted seas, beyond our horizon..."

TO THE HOMEWARD ISLES

Shout-laughing in a crazed frenzy
I yanked my flukes from earthen moors
Hoisted full canvas to the sky
Lost all vision of foreign shores

Setting course to the Homeward Isles
With winds abaft and running free
Ignoring every darkening cloud
That sailed within four points of me

My sloop not more than a shadow
Close-hulled on life's immortal sea
Tacking down the honeyed coastline
Into my God's eternity.....

O' STARRY NIGHT

A mad-whirling cartwheeling of lights
Slow flashes white above my head as
Life stars in the heavens go wild—sucked
Down the big black hole like millions of
Hot lightning bugs in an August night.

Van Gogh, you well knew the starry night
And that insanity, alone, is
Not enough to chain a man; it takes
All God has to make the locks stick tight.

I anchor my body to the ground,
Bolt it to this reeling, spinning star
Spread my legs for better balance, then
Let it whirl me onward, whip me hard
Cartwheeling off to nowhere from the
Womb of time into infinity.

You who have taken this strange voyage
Won't you lend me confidence to sail
This black ship into the great unknown?
O' mother, at last I'm coming home!
My brother Van Gogh, hold out your hand
And wait for me beyond the stars for
Like you, I was a child of the sun...
Once it smiled on me, toasted my skin
Gave substance, for awhile, to my bread
Until it baked the clay into red plates
Squinting its rayed eyes into my soul!

One must give something for the exchange
With grace and thanksgiving, and so I
Hand it back hilt first on bended knee,
My debt fully paid: accept my soul
As it is, weathered inside time's cage.

bits

bits of youth
bits of love
bits of life
and...tomorrow
bits of sorrow
bits of maturity
bits of wisdom
bits of aging
...and finally
lots of dying
recycling bits

THE WINCE OF FIFTY

The wince of fifty,
The facial blanche,
An epiphany of age...
I didn't think I'd live so long.

A collection of years
To rely upon...
To charge all things to
Experience already experienced.

How shall I say
That I'm growing old?
Looks are deceiving,
Feelings, no longer reliable.

...I want to erase the tape
To start a new recording,
And then I think of...nothing.

SONG TO A SONG AT FORTY-EIGHT

I have finished my bath and I think—
I'm in pretty good shape! Well, maybe
A little flabby in some places,
But, I feel I'm in pretty good shape.

I look down at myself—proud flesh
I have had, and still have a little,
As my mind shoots questions to my warm
And open pores, "How much of me is
Dying; how much is already dead?"

"How long will it be until all of
My toe nails grow out, curl under, and
Grow back into my flesh and make me
More irritable? I'll cut them now—
But," I wonder, "Who will cut them later?"

Putrid thought runs on and on—over
Putrid flesh—holding on to places,
Times, and people. My naked self sees
No disgrace in living the way its
Soul intended it to live, as I
Sing a song to a "Song of Myself"
At forty-eight...I rebuke the whole
Civilized world for its inferences...
I grow a beard today...and wear it
To my grave, to keep my dignity.

Song to a "Song of Myself": Thou shalt
Not impinge, thou shalt not trudge...upon
This naked self, this private soul, for
My naked self belongs to me, Sirs!
Thou shalt not! Thou shalt not! Thou shalt not!

BETTER TO DIE FREE

Too many seasons he had cheated death,
Found himself tumbling out of control but
Then what had it mattered in these late years
If a chance had been taken there or here
When he had learned he had loved too well and
The true essence of life was swept away
Until the balancing weight read zero?
Finished, he sought the priest of the nightshade,
Met him in the mountains, made a pact, and
Took the road less traveled, determined to
Pay his debt for having lived so freely:
"Better to die free with an unenslaved
Mind and spirit than one so encumbered
And preoccupied by earthly snares," said
He, running headlong toward the open pass.
The mountains aptly had supported his
Philosophy, had made him stronger than
His deepest years so he could well afford
The user fees required to keep him free.

OR WAS IT JUST
THE FIRST CRASH OF MY SOUL?

Very late, late in the year, near the
Slow turn of the winter, I first sensed a
Turning of the earth, felt it whirl and swirl
Beneath my feet, within my head...or,
Was it just some kidney stones, stacking up an
Outlet, or my spleen splattering red, or my
Bladder spilling chartreuse...More, or less?

The moment strummed with cutting, biting sounds
Of windy strings set in deep throated harps.
Stars stricken by a frozen sky stared
Sternly down. All this I could see and feel,
Mixed in the rolling white light unbalancing
My footing and my composition...
Moving backward to an uprising west-
Setting moon, contrary to pattern,
·I thought, ''Oh, God, it should go the other way!''

When was it last I'd felt it so alive?
When was it last I'd watched it move? Was it
The thrust-rushing of the St. Lawrence, eroding
A continent before my very eyes?
Or, the fire-spitting Stromboli, rolling molten
Lava into the sizzling sea before me?
Or, was it just the first crash of my soul
Into an outstretched mountain of reality?

SO ISN'T IT?

So isn't it too bad
That it's not good enough
This life...
Good enough
To make men want to Live
Instead of Dying?

A LATE YEAR FLIGHT

I saw a man look down upon this world
As I had never seen a man look down
Before; I saw him search beyond his grave.
We saw the same rivers, mountains, roads, and
Houses that we both had seen before; yet
Something in his grey gaze this time would have
Said to any poet: "Hey, there!" and I should
Have said, "What? Why are you thinking that way?
There's more and more to see along the way.
Hell! That's no sacred spot! Let's not stop there today.
We'll have another go-a-round and bounce
Gracefully, if you please, a time or two
It will make little difference what the Doctor
Has to say today!" But, I couldn't say
A word: I saw tears welling in his eyes
And I thought of what it's like for a bird
To lose its wings. It would be the old
Eagle's last flight. And then I remembered,
"He's soloed before! He's not afraid!"

THE SHORTEST WEIGHT

Through eons of time, man all the while
    dangles like a weight
Suspended only by the strength of
    one slim silken strand
Some mistaken spider spun in a
    spur of urgency
And in a self-same selfishness to
    locate the prey...here
Suspended...each man hangs, alone, to
    dangle to and fro
Caught in slender shafts of silent light
    amidst uncounted
Billions of lightyears whose beginnings
    and endings can be
Distinguished no more than that instant
    segment in which man
Calculates his lifespan along some
    indefinite path
Called eternity—at most, he has
    a day or a night,
A few seasons or seconds—the length
    is but the same for
Each must say goodbye to all he knows
    to all the things that
He had never really dreamed of—through
    no fault of his own;
He learned to laugh, and he learned to cry,
    the latter much more
Difficult for his nature and the
    greater feat, by far.

THE DEATH WISH

I have traveled down many a road
Fully expecting to meet my fate
At every bend and wondering
When I did not
Still, there's consolation in knowing
My life is half past the hour and
Our meeting here or there will not be
Unexpected.

There was a day when all of my life
Was rich and well
And I was the holder of the keys
To an open door called "Happiness"
But then it passed
Like the waning of the moon, and all
My wealth was gone—leaving me stranded
High and dry—on the awful bar of
Reality.

> After the death of a son
> 24 June 1964

SUMMER SORROW

I wept at twenty and four
At thirty and six so much more
Another time (I don't remember when)
But summer never came to me again.

THE RITUAL OF LOVE

The dancers had ceased their whirl about
The small green leaves were chewed and swallowed
The ritual was made complete
With the bestowing of the name.
The name, that ancient name that was
Bestowed upon the little son,
O' how important it must have been
Yet, it cannot be recalled now
For, then, life was too much a dream;
The meaning was to Indians, a
Name for silver chains and golden clasps
That bind two hearts and make them one,
It bound the father and the son.

Only a pale face, one-eighth, they said
Descended from a Cherokee squaw,
Hungett from Reed Creek heritage.
We understood little of it then,
He, the faithful son, true and loyal
I, the father, proud and humbled;
But with the passing of the years,
The wooded morning reappears
High in these everlasting hills
And we stand overlooking bliss—
A jaded world of heavy oak
Gnarled and tried by winter winds—
Father sealed to son again.

ACT IV SCENE V

No frogs to croak
No birds to sing
No sunny days
Of freshest spring.

No setting sun
Or western sky
No apple red
To please the eye.

No trout to hook
No plums to grow
No blooms to shed
In blowing snow
To move the mind
From what it knows
.....Stage left.

AMBER EVENING GLOW

It hurts to know
That it is time for
Amber evening glow,
The dusk of life
Before the night

The daylight is too short
To see what is, should be
You walk this way but once
On silver shaded paths
Beneath the elder trees
Till crimson leaves of fall
Brown in December's
Amber evening glow

Yours last evening, love
And mine, today
The silence of
Our amber evening glow

DEATH MUST BE...

Life is a puff of dust
    twisting in the road
    before you,
Caught for a moment in
    the beam of your
    headlights,
Then whisked upward
    and away.....

Why, I think
    that death
    must
    be
    a
    holiday.

THE GOODNIGHT OF THE FUGITIVE

A pearl pestle of soft winds pulverize
Stellar light with wild honeysuckle bloom
In a mortar of velvet night blending
A succulent scent and suffocating
The scintillating bard—paying him, the
Apothecary fugitive, for his
Toil, his life's strivings. Nodding now, having
Communed with the elements more than most,
The fugitive sleeps, dreaming slow like the
Drop of a midnight sun that waits to go.

30 December 1973

WHEN I THINK OF MY FRIENDS LIVING AND DEAD

When I think of my friends who have died
Whose gentle faces are now looking upward
Or downward, as it may be defined
Whose dreams of life here on this earth were
Laid aside, and some suddenly so, for
Greater adventures on the other side,
I think of their smiles, their hearty laughter
Now all stilled by the grim Death Stalker
And I count the number of my friends dead
Greater than the number of my friends alive;
And as I think of them, I think of man's feeble
Effort here on earth toward happiness
And peace of mind, and what little meaning
Life holds without it; and I think of this,
When I think of my friends living and dead,
We are all made slaves by our society
More surely, more securely, than if planned.

LEFT ALL BEHIND

Tell them I was killed by a poison dart
Someone I knew let fly—
Barbed with the mind and dark from the heart
Too venomed to go by.
That's why I could not, as they said, "Be a man!"
So I leaped across a deep gorge of time,
Shedded myself as I went. Left all behind.

A KING HAS FALLEN

My mother's dead, my father's dying
With one leg less already
Lost in a battle to the Turks;
My last young wife is growing old
It's obvious to my senses,
Ranting between the battle walls
Shall I go searching for another?
This hearth-sitting's getting to me!
Shall I sail to a far-off place
And think of things I've never thought,
Take my mind off the war? before?
Shall I try not to feel the knee
That hurts only when it rains, or
Try not to notice the strain in
My stride, the change that strikes a tone
Of finality to the hard
Transition of a strong young man
To an old and feeble one, that
Awkwardness that reverberates
Like the sound of a giant gong
To outer edges of this soul,
Or shall I go in search of heaven,
Mother to my wives and fifty sons?

MESSAGE TO APOLLO

O' Polyhymnia, intercede
Straightway with winged feet to Apollo!
Say that my friend is dead and I mourn
For one so rare in these late years, that
I call not directly upon him
Because I am both blind and halt and
So unworthy compared to my friend,
Unable to approach his shining
Presence on the great Olympic plain.

Sing, o' Muse of Arcadia,
Sing a song of everflowing love
A boundless isthmus on this sea of time;
Sing not of summer joys but of the
Searing flesh and burning fevers that
Come with the thought of the great waste the
Death reaper shocks at my hovel door;
Tell him I weep for my weathered friend
Who moves not under the blue sky or
Beneath the golden sun, moves no more
Inside the wind or rain, moves no more!

Invoke aid to this heart-rending song,
Tell that I am one who has remained
True to the gods of old, that even
Now I go to render homage;
Instruct me in the delightful flow
Of honeyed words to form a fitting
Monument to such a wondrous creature
That the ruins may be savored
With other past and future splendors
Not in vain defamation, but in
Glorious remembrance of his life
In these green hills of Arcadia.

Requiem

REQUIEM TO A COMRADE

Hard were the battles you fought, my friend, and
For so long a time as each engagement
Became more puzzling and the strategists
Could not say what would be the best tactic
Though they tried on every hand and failed
To make heads or tails of the terrible
Malady, this thing that overtook you,
The delirium that weighted you down,
Ate deep within you, until at long last
Near the end, they were afraid to say while
You paid in blood for their cures, the new and
The old brought to your door; still the thing grew
With long-reaching tendrils scaling the walls
Of an otherwise beautiful mind and
Raced through the night like those fire-spitting
Cannonballs on the old Wabash Railroad
That you knew so well in your youth and where
You gave signals of red, green, and amber
Coloring lives depending on you and
Your deep strong affection for metallic
Charges shared only with those you loved most
Made us far less afraid of the awesome
Dark creatures that keep moving toward us
In the unreeling cinema of life...
And when your mind spewed fire, steam, and cinders
Along the rocky road bed, when the twin
Rails and crossties tormentedly bolted
In too swift derailment, when all of us
Here who cared deeply about you could no
Longer interpret your waybill of routes,
When society itself offered so
Little assistance from a government
Which formulates what ought to become the
Proper perspective toward frail human frames

And, instead, it became the cruel hunting
Animal in your gentle eyes, preying
Upon the poor, sick, and the blind—when all
Of this happened, you left us, to ponder.....

In my thoughts of you and my thoughts of life,
This mind surges on an impatient sea...

To the days of our youth when you were so
Strong, when we both were so healthy and as
Handsome as hell! and chose to go sailing
The great ships of our nation in the name
Of our country, our God, and our freedom,
Asking little of others and giving
All of ourselves for a small, token wage...

To the days of bright sparkling waters and
Blinding rich sunlight that buoyed the isles
Like smooth-floating jewels in their moistened
Jade crystals that carried our ship into
All the tomorrows of times yet unlived
In uncharted seas, beyond our horizon...

To the brown satin lasses bearing iced
Rainbow sherbets in tropical hours
And the rope-yarn Sundays we chose to
Languish on shore, roasting in silence like
Two giant turtles of ancient sea lore...

To the trembling girls who fed lusty
Young appetites strong, feisty drinks under
Palms swaying gently in the cool of the
Evening on stretches of powdery sand...

To the blue-white of moonlight flooding the
Shores and the ships in soft, breaking seas to

Requiem

Herald the haunting of incessant songs
Murmuring moods in our minds and prompting
Strange apparitions to dance to and fro
On near and far distant seascapes, in a
Melange of colors and spectrum of forms
That stated true measure of voices and
Bodies trapped in the silvery silence
Of many life-filled compartments below...

To the high speed of ships that skimmed on cool
Silken paths, fluorescently lit like the
Great Northern Sky, harboring tons of fresh
Sea life teeming below and making these
Travels the happiest days of our lives...

To the stalk of bananas we hoisted
Up to the signal halyards of that old
Destroyer, the stalk we'd walked off with from
The loading dock below, when the Captain
Caught us two-blocking it to the signal
Bridge and he just laughed, with eyes wondering
What in the hell we'd be doing with a
Tree of bananas behind his cabin...

To the sailor who married his car, how
He beat her up the nights that he drank just
To repair and polish her love-ing-ly
The mornings after, insisting that the
Blame was all due to those tricky "one-eyed
Indians" he had drunk the night before...

Some years later, when you and I had had
Our fill of those high seatime adventures,
We both had come back to roots of farmsoil,
Yours on the midwestern plain, mine on the

Hills of the Blue Ridge chain—to labor and
Think and go off to college to learn more
About the world we'd sailed over, all the
Great ports and nations and peoples we'd seen;
And inbetween the tight-fitted schedules,
You came rushing across America
To my graduation...and I think how
Lucky I am to have had such a friend,
Such a true friend in you...and it's strange how
It seems that of all of the people I
Have ever encountered, you seemed to be
Always measuring your days, tasting the
Present delights against the ones that were
Never to be, taking advantage of
The little time you had to live...and when
I compare my life to yours, I feel so
Unconscious, yet you knew all along I
Suppose...is that why you tried hard to wrap
Everything up by 1983...
How did you know? Is that why certain years
In the future have ways of haunting me?
Which year will be the farewell one to see?
Yet, I'm most gleeful for the days I was
Blessed knowing you and am still happier
Than I am sick at heart...and so I sing
My friend, all the songs that we knew and once
Sang together, yet facing the fact that
Alone, most of the fun is now gone.

How I find joy in your juvenescence
Of style—that bubbling contagion in your
Boyish smile, in your soft voice subduing
The musical scale, content as a brook
Singing after a flood, in your gleaming

Requiem

Eyes changing colors each day from hazel
To blue, dark brown, and then grey—all this you
Shared freely with others as long as you
Lived, with never an expectation of
Some returning gift for you never spent
Your friends, you saved them for their tomorrows
And gave more life to them in the knowing.

Knowing you in such gracious exchanges
Sharing those unblighted gems of our youth
And observing your sweet gentle nature
Available to all for the gleaning
Was the most beautiful experience;
And I believe you will always be a
Part of the true nature and reflected
In every act of those your life touched;
And you should know that since your passing, we've
All mourned you in our separate ways, yet
We have all blamed ourselves for not doing
More for you and blamed you for leaving us!

I have no thought where you are now, Comrade,
Though I meekly accept your past scoldings
For my restless doubts concerning such an
Unimaginable thing as a place
For souls after this life, yet whatever
There is for those you left behind, we'll be
Hard pressed to approach the place of splendor
That had to be reserved for you alone.

I had to follow in your last footsteps...
Retracing the lonely trail of your lost
Desires, seeing firsthand the manifold
Colors of the ripped fabric of your worn
Reclusive soul, the place where you slept and

Lived alone in that upper room, and I
Realized just how completely you had
Thrown yourself into that endless spiral
Of the Heart of Darkness, to so fully
Withdraw from all you knew; I understood,
Comrade, I suffered with you and a bit
Of my soul slipped away in your going—
In terrible loss of a work of art
Newly found, in the ultimate ruins
Of a man, an art that could never be,
For man is against himself—refuses
To honor his own greatness and just hands
It all back to some imaginary
Entity in a one-sided worship.

Yet, I would have you see emphatically
That you were loved intensely for yourself
By all who knew your gentle, placid soul,
You were loved with an ample love few men
Ever experience in this life and
I, your friend and old comrade in arms, stand
Witness to this rich shared bond, and we who
Loved you have done the best we could, trying
To learn to live again, though it's been a
Most difficult chore and still incomplete.

For a long while, I sat isolated;
People were disturbed by my death pallor,
My incomprehensible attitude,
My inability to place my feet
One before the other without tripping
Off an awkward, stumbling gate...over time
I am coming to accept what must be,
To know what life is with trimmings removed,
To see how terribly alone we walk.

Requiem

Bitter at your parting, I held God the
Suspect in a useless, hideous crime,
An outrageous joke on all of us, on
Me because in you I'd found the fifty
Sons spent at Troy and I mourn you with a
Heathen hurt in my eyes and breast that can
No longer understand nor will it change,
Another blue unhealing fall wound and
Not knowing the reason for such riddles,
The need for such puzzling waste, I've found the
Burden far too great for I cannot be
The youthful blond of yesterday's isles
Laughing to the sea and sky, nor will I
Likely change from my black morning mood for
I am not a Milton and this is not
The age or place to try to justify
The ways of God to man, but how deeply
I regret the losing of any found
Paradise, and so I go not gentle
Into the night, I mourn Troy along with
Old King Priam and Hecuba and for
My fifty sons, my shipmate, my brother,
I rage "against the dying of the light."

Your last thoughts to me were of a purple
Thanksgiving for soft summer rain and for
A friendship untarnished by the years, still
In the scattering of your ashes, I
Can only return a splintered heart and
Know at some appointed hour I, too,
Will add my ashes to that now growing
Sea-like heap, the gathering of my sons
And friends, my blood coming home, and if I
Wail the awful human howl during dark
Winter nights, it is but to ask that you
Wait for me, for in each dusk I see a
Ship preparing to keep a rendezvous......

DON'S BLUE FORD

My pal had a thing for blue Fords
And perhaps other designer
Technicians produced this car craze;
It might have stemmed from just knowing
His favorite grandfather on
A Nokomis, Illinois farm
Had sold him his '39 coupe
(After their first exchange of a
Treasured '33 Model A).

The blue had spunk and Don raced it
In stocks with coordinated,
Mechanically dexterous skill
Yet couldn't learn how Genny could
Squeal wheels without even trying
One thing he still envied in vain!
When he converted the inside
Into a small highway camper,
He toured America in it,
Telling me he was awakened
One night in some faraway place
From deeply sound sleep—encircled
By floodlights and the law screaming
At him to "Give up and come out!"

An LTD 1969
Another beloved blue Ford
Was my buddy's pride and sweet joy,
"A man's car" beautiful in its
Midnight and fine-polished thick chrome.
Stickers proclaimed a travelogue
By sailor and soldier loving
His country, visiting places
Some only dream of sightseeing...

Don's Blue Ford

Paddling the Mississippi on
The Delta Queen to New Orleans,
Williamsburg and the history
He admired, with Independence
'76 Bicentennial
Plates updated to '82
And, "Virginia Is For Lovers"...
I remember him writing how
He'd worn out his first set of shoes
In his adopted mountain state
And seemed to be proud of the fact.

A transportation addict from
Fine blue wheels to walking leather
He saw it all and gave us back
A blithe spirit of adventure!

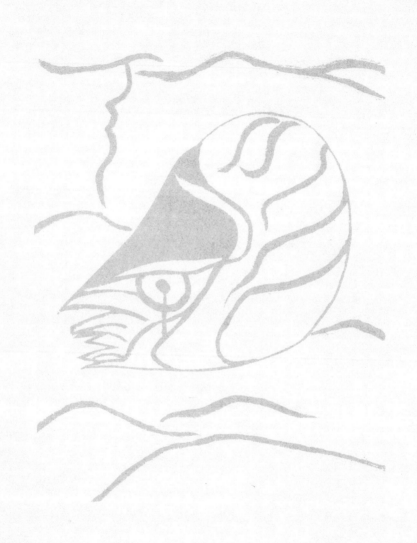